CONTENTS

ABRAHAM LINCOLN

Abraham Lincoln was the sixteenth U.S. president. He was the son of poor farmers. Lincoln did not receive much formal education. But, he loved reading and read every book he could find.

As a young man, Lincoln held many jobs. When he was just 25, he won election to the Illinois state legislature. During this time, he studied to be a lawyer. Later, Lincoln served in the U.S. House of Representatives. There, he spoke out against slavery.

In 1861, Lincoln became president. As president, he led the country through the worst war ever fought in the United States. This was the American Civil War. Eventually, the North defeated the South.

Sadly, President Lincoln did not get to see his country peacefully reunited. Just a few days after the Civil War ended, Lincoln was **assassinated**. Lincoln had worked to preserve the country and end slavery. Today, many people regard him as the greatest leader in U.S. history.

TIMELINE

1809 - On February 12, Abraham Lincoln was born in Hodgenville, Kentucky.

1832 - Lincoln served in the Black Hawk War; he campaigned for a seat in the Illinois state legislature, but lost.

1833 - In May, Lincoln was appointed postmaster of New Salem, Illinois; that fall, he began serving as deputy county surveyor.

1834 - Lincoln won a seat in the Illinois state legislature.

1842 - On November 4, Lincoln married Mary Ann Todd.

1847 - Lincoln began serving in the U.S. House of Representatives.

1856 - Lincoln joined the newly formed Republican Party.

1858 - While running for the U.S. Senate, Lincoln debated Senator Stephen A. Douglas; Lincoln lost the election.

1860 - On November 6, Lincoln was elected the sixteenth U.S. president; on December 20, South Carolina became the first Southern state to secede from the Union.

1861 - In January, South Carolina and six other Southern states formed the Confederate States of America; on March 4, Lincoln was inaugurated president; the Confederacy attacked Fort Sumter on April 12, starting the American Civil War.

1863 - On January 1, President Lincoln issued the Emancipation Proclamation; Lincoln delivered the Gettysburg Address on November 19.

1865 - Congress passed the Thirteenth Amendment; Lincoln began his second term in March; the American Civil War ended; on April 14, John Wilkes Booth shot President Lincoln; Abraham Lincoln died on April 15.

DID YOU KNOW?

Abraham Lincoln was the tallest U.S. president. He stood six feet four inches (1.9 m) tall.

Lincoln was strong and skilled with an ax. He was sometimes called "the Rail-Splitter." Even in his later years, Lincoln could hold an ax straight out at arm's length. Few young men could do the same.

Lincoln is one of the most recognized faces in U.S. history. He appears on the nation's one cent coin and five dollar bill. Lincoln is also one of four presidents carved on Mount Rushmore in South Dakota.

The Lincoln Memorial in Washington, D.C., was dedicated on May 30, 1922. It had taken eight years to construct. Thirty-six columns surround the building. They represent the number of U.S. states at the time of Lincoln's death.

PRESIDENT OF THE
POTUS
UNITED STATES

A Modest Start

Abraham Lincoln was born in Hodgenville, Kentucky, on February 12, 1809. He was the second child of Thomas and Nancy Lincoln. Abraham's older sister was named Sarah. His younger brother, Thomas, died as a baby.

Abraham grew up living in log cabins. The Lincoln family was poor, but they were close. In 1811, they moved to a farm at Knob Creek, Kentucky. Abraham helped with many chores on the farm. He chopped wood, planted crops, and carried water. When Abraham wasn't working, he liked to explore the nearby woods and climb the cliffs.

When Abraham turned six, he began his education. However, he was often needed on the farm. So, he could only attend school occasionally. Abraham learned reading, writing, and mathematics. He liked writing best. Abraham practiced anywhere he could.

FAST FACTS

BORN - February 12, 1809
WIFE - Mary Ann Todd (1818–1882)
CHILDREN - 4
POLITICAL PARTY - Republican
AGE AT INAUGURATION - 52
YEARS SERVED - 1861–1865
VICE PRESIDENTS - Hannibal Hamlin, Andrew Johnson
DIED - April 15, 1865, age 56

The Lincoln family moved to Indiana in December 1816. Abraham and his father worked hard to build a new home there. Then in October 1818, Nancy Lincoln died. The next year, Abraham's father married a woman named Sarah Bush Johnston.

Sarah soon noticed that Abraham liked to learn. He was especially interested in reading. Sometimes he walked miles to find a new book. Sarah encouraged Abraham's love of books and helped him continue his education.

At night, Abraham sat near the fire to read by its light. He read the Bible, *Aesop's Fables,* and Robinson Crusoe.

HONEST ABE

*When Lincoln moved to New Salem, Illinois,
it was a village of about 25 families.*

Lincoln grew to be tall and strong. When he was old enough, he got a job **ferrying** passengers across the Ohio River. Then in 1828, Lincoln took his first trip away from Indiana. He helped drive a boat down the Mississippi River to New Orleans, Louisiana.

In March 1830, Lincoln's family moved to Illinois. There, Lincoln worked as a store clerk in New Salem. In April 1832, he

Lincoln served a total of 90 days in the militia.

decided to run for the Illinois state legislature. But before he could begin campaigning, the **Black Hawk War** broke out.

Lincoln wanted to help fight in the war. So, he joined the Illinois state **militia**. Lincoln was made a captain. But, he did not fight in any battles.

Lincoln returned to New Salem in July. Just two weeks remained before the Illinois elections. Lincoln did not win. Even so, he had earned most of the votes from his own **precinct**.

After his loss, Lincoln opened a store with his friend William Berry. However, the store quickly went out of business. Then in May 1833, Lincoln was appointed New Salem's **postmaster**. That fall, he also began serving as **deputy county surveyor**. Lincoln worked hard and earned a reputation for honesty. Soon, people began calling him "Honest Abe."

LAW AND MARRIAGE

In 1834, Lincoln again ran for the Illinois state legislature. This time he won! He went on to win the next three elections. By 1836, Lincoln had become a leader of the **Whig** Party.

While in office, Lincoln worked to move Illinois's capital from Vandalia to Springfield. He supported constructing railroads and canals. This would improve the state's transportation system. Lincoln also helped establish the Bank of Illinois.

In his free time, Lincoln studied law. On September 9, 1836, he received his law license. Then in April 1837, he moved to Springfield. Lincoln quickly established a successful law practice. He handled cases for businesses such as railroads, banks, and factories.

In winter 1839, Lincoln attended a dance in Springfield. There, he met a young woman named Mary Ann Todd. She was well educated. They both loved poetry and shared an interest in politics.

On November 4, 1842, the couple married. The Lincolns later had four children. They welcomed Robert Todd in 1843 and Edward in 1846. William followed in 1850. Thomas, called Tad, was born in 1853.

Mary Todd Lincoln

A NEW PARTY

In 1846, Lincoln ran for a seat in the U.S. House of Representatives. He won the election and began serving on March 4, 1847.

In Congress, Lincoln fought against slavery. He proposed a law to free slaves in Washington, D.C. It said the government would pay slave owners to release their slaves. But, Lincoln's law did not pass.

Lincoln also fought against the **Mexican War**. He believed it had been started for the wrong reasons. So, Lincoln challenged President James K. Polk's motives for going to war. Lincoln's actions angered many people.

When the United States won the Mexican War, Mexico gave up much land. Lincoln did not want slavery there. So, he voted for a law called the

James K. Polk was president from 1845 to 1849.

14

Wilmot Proviso. It proposed banning slavery in the territories gained from Mexico. However, this law did not pass.

Lincoln did not run for reelection to Congress. In 1849, he returned to his law practice. The next year, the Lincolns suffered a personal tragedy. Their son Edward died. He was just four years old.

Meanwhile, the **Whig** Party lost support and soon died out. In its place, the **Republican** Party formed to oppose the spread of slavery.

In 1856, Lincoln joined the new party. He helped organize the Illinois branch and soon became a party leader there.

The Lincolns moved into their Springfield home in May 1844.
They raised their family there for 17 years.

A HOUSE DIVIDED

For many years, Americans had argued about whether or not to allow slavery. In 1858, **Republicans** nominated Lincoln to run for the U.S. Senate. In his acceptance speech Lincoln said, "A house divided against itself cannot stand." He believed the nation could not last if it was divided over slavery.

Lincoln ran against **Democrat** Stephen A. Douglas, who held the Senate seat. Lincoln challenged Douglas to participate in a series

Lincoln and Douglas debated seven times in locations around Illinois.

of **debates** with him. Their arguments centered on the extension of slavery.

During the debates, Lincoln spoke against allowing slavery in new territories. Douglas supported allowing territories to choose whether to allow slavery.

Lincoln lost the election. Yet, he gained national attention.

A campaign poster from the 1860 election

On May 18, 1860, **Republican** Party leaders nominated Lincoln for president. Senator Hannibal Hamlin of Maine became his **running mate**.

The **Democratic** Party was split. So, Northern Democrats nominated Douglas, and Southern Democrats nominated Vice President John C. Breckinridge. The **Constitutional Union Party** nominated former senator John Bell of Tennessee.

On November 6, Lincoln won the election with 180 electoral votes. Breckinridge received 92, Bell earned 39, and Douglas won just 12.

ROAD TO WAR

The Southern states depended on slavery. They felt a **Republican** president would threaten their way of life. So on December 20, 1860, South Carolina **seceded**. It became the first state to secede from the **Union**.

The United States during the American Civil War

Fort Sumter was established as a national monument in 1948.

To keep other states from **seceding**, Congress proposed the Crittenden Compromise. It said slavery would stay legal in existing slave states. And, territories would be equally divided into slave and free territories. But, the law did not pass.

In January 1861, six more states seceded. They were Alabama, Florida, Georgia, Louisiana, Mississippi, and Texas. Together with South Carolina, they formed the Confederate States of America. Arkansas, North Carolina, Tennessee, and Virginia eventually joined the Confederacy as well.

In February, the Lincolns were heartbroken when their son William died. Then on March 4, Lincoln was **inaugurated** president. In his inaugural address, he stated his desire to preserve the nation. Yet, the Southern states remained unhappy.

Meanwhile, Fort Sumter in South Carolina was still under federal power. The Confederacy demanded U.S. troops abandon the fort. The troops refused, so the Confederacy attacked the fort on April 12. Soon after, Lincoln called for volunteers to join the **Union** army. The American Civil War had begun.

HOPE FOR THE FUTURE

Meanwhile, Lincoln had spent much time thinking about the war and slavery. He felt slavery was wrong. Yet, he believed the U.S. **Constitution** protected slavery where it already existed.

However, President Lincoln also believed America stood for freedom and equality. So, he did not want slavery to spread. Lincoln decided to add a new goal to the war. In addition to reuniting the United States, he wanted to end slavery.

Yet, Lincoln worried that immediately freeing all slaves might cause the border states to **secede**. These states were Kentucky, Missouri, Delaware, and Maryland. They allowed slavery but had remained part of the **Union**.

So, President Lincoln came up with a plan. On September 22, 1862, he issued an announcement. It stated that all slaves in the Confederate states would be freed by the next year.

Then on January 1, 1863, President Lincoln issued the Emancipation Proclamation. It announced that all slaves in the Confederate states were now free.

The Emancipation Proclamation

Lincoln hoped the border states would choose to free their slaves. However, they did not. Still, slavery was coming to an end. Lincoln became known as the Great Emancipator.

The Emancipation Proclamation also announced President Lincoln's decision to use African-American troops. About 180,000 African Americans served in the **Union** army. Two-thirds of them were former slaves who had fled the South.

Lincoln wrote five versions of his famous Gettysburg Address.

In March 1863, President Lincoln signed a law that created military **conscription**. This strengthened the **Union**'s military forces. The North began to take control of the war.

That July, Union forces won the Battle of Gettysburg in Pennsylvania. It was the only battle fought on Northern soil. On November 19, the battlefield was honored as a national cemetery. President Lincoln gave a speech during the ceremony.

Lincoln's Gettysburg Address was short but powerful. He said, "The government of the people, by the people, for the people, shall not perish from the earth." Lincoln's speech gave people hope for the future. And, it inspired them to keep the United States together.

Meanwhile, Western Virginia had **seceded** from Confederate Virginia in June 1861. West Virginia was admitted to the United States on June 20, 1863. Nevada became a state the following year.

PRESIDENT LINCOLN'S CABINET

FIRST TERM
MARCH 4, 1861–MARCH 4, 1865

- **STATE –** William H. Seward
- **TREASURY –** Salmon P. Chase
  William P. Fessenden (from July 5, 1864)
- **WAR –** Simon Cameron
  Edwin M. Stanton (from June 20, 1862)
- **NAVY –** Gideon Welles
- **ATTORNEY GENERAL –** Edward Bates
  James Speed (from December 5, 1864)
- **INTERIOR –** Caleb B. Smith
  John P. Usher (from January 8, 1863)

SECOND TERM
MARCH 4, 1865–APRIL 15, 1865

- **STATE –** William H. Seward
- **TREASURY –** Hugh McCulloch
- **WAR –** Edwin M. Stanton
- **NAVY –** Gideon Welles
- **ATTORNEY GENERAL –** James Speed
- **INTERIOR –** John P. Usher

FIGHTING FOR PEACE

In March 1864, Lincoln promoted Grant to lieutenant general. He also gave Grant command of all the federal armies. Later that year, the **Union** secured several victories in the South. The Confederacy was losing the war.

Vice President Andrew Johnson took office as president after Lincoln's death.

Also in 1864, **Republicans** and some **Democrats** who supported Lincoln joined together as the Union Party. They renominated Lincoln for president. Democrat and former senator Andrew Johnson became his **running mate**. The Democratic Party nominated former general George B. McClellan. His running mate was Representative George H. Pendleton of Ohio.

Union victories in the war helped Lincoln win reelection. He earned 212 electoral votes to McClellan's 21.

Northerners were now certain they would win the war. So, President Lincoln began making plans for **Reconstruction**.

Meanwhile, Lincoln supported the Thirteenth **Amendment**. It would ban slavery in the United States. In January 1865, Congress passed the amendment. It was then sent to the states to be **ratified**.

In March 1865, Lincoln took office for the second time. Then on April 9, Confederate general Robert E. Lee surrendered to General Grant. They met in Appomattox Court House, Virginia. At last, the Civil War was over.

The Thirteenth Amendment became part of the U.S. Constitution in December 1865.

A TRAGIC ENDING

After shooting Lincoln, Booth leaped onto the stage. He shouted, "The South is avenged!"

Finally, it seemed the nation would have peace. Then on April 14, 1865, tragedy struck. President Lincoln and his wife went to Ford's Theatre in Washington, D.C. They attended the play *Our American Cousin*.

During the play, John Wilkes Booth snuck into Lincoln's theater box. Booth was a Confederate supporter. He was upset that the South had lost the Civil War.

At 10:22 PM, Booth shot Lincoln in the back of the head. The president was rushed to a boardinghouse across the street. Several doctors tried to save his life. But, Abraham Lincoln died the next day at 7:22 AM.

On April 26, Booth was captured and killed in Virginia. Others involved in the plot to kill the president surrendered. They were found guilty of murder. Some went to jail for life, and others were executed.

The nation was shocked at the **assassination** of President Lincoln. Thousands mourned his death. A train carried his body from Washington, D.C., to Springfield. There, he was buried in the Oak Ridge Cemetery.

Lincoln was a strong, compassionate leader. He led the country through the dark days of civil war. He worked to end slavery and preserve the United States. These accomplishments made Abraham Lincoln one of America's most important presidents.

OFFICE OF THE PRESIDENT

BRANCHES OF GOVERNMENT

The U.S. government is divided into three branches. They are the executive, legislative, and judicial branches. This division is called a separation of powers. Each branch has some power over the others. This is called a system of checks and balances.

EXECUTIVE BRANCH

The executive branch enforces laws. It is made up of the president, the vice president, and the president's cabinet. The president represents the United States around the world. He or she oversees relations with other countries and signs treaties. The president signs bills into law and appoints officials and federal judges. He or she also leads the military and manages government workers.

LEGISLATIVE BRANCH

The legislative branch makes laws, maintains the military, and regulates trade. It also has the power to declare war. This branch consists of the Senate and the House of Representatives. Together, these two houses make up Congress. Each state has two senators. A state's population determines the number of representatives it has.

JUDICIAL BRANCH

The judicial branch interprets laws. It consists of district courts, courts of appeals, and the Supreme Court. District courts try cases. If a person disagrees with a trial's outcome, he or she may appeal. If the courts of appeals support the ruling, a person may appeal to the Supreme Court. The Supreme Court also makes sure that laws follow the U.S. Constitution.

QUALIFICATIONS FOR OFFICE

To be president, a person must meet three requirements. A candidate must be at least 35 years old and a natural-born U.S. citizen. He or she must also have lived in the United States for at least 14 years.

ELECTORAL COLLEGE

The U.S. presidential election is an indirect election. Voters from each state choose electors to represent them in the Electoral College. The number of electors from each state is based on population. Each elector has one electoral vote. Electors are pledged to cast their vote for the candidate who receives the highest number of popular votes in their state. A candidate must receive the majority of Electoral College votes to win.

TERM OF OFFICE

Each president may be elected to two four-year terms. Sometimes, a president may only be elected once. This happens if he or she served more than two years of the previous president's term.

The presidential election is held on the Tuesday after the first Monday in November. The president is sworn in on January 20 of the following year. At that time, he or she takes the oath of office:

I do solemnly swear (or affirm) that I will faithfully execute the office of President of the United States, and will to the best of my ability, preserve, protect and defend the Constitution of the United States.

LINE OF SUCCESSION

The Presidential Succession Act of 1947 defines who becomes president if the president cannot serve. The vice president is first in the line of succession. Next are the Speaker of the House and the President Pro Tempore of the Senate. If none of these individuals is able to serve, the office falls to the president's cabinet members. They would take office in the order in which each department was created:

Secretary of State

Secretary of the Treasury

Secretary of Defense

Attorney General

Secretary of the Interior

Secretary of Agriculture

Secretary of Commerce

Secretary of Labor

Secretary of Health and Human Services

Secretary of Housing and Urban Development

Secretary of Transportation

Secretary of Energy

Secretary of Education

Secretary of Veterans Affairs

Secretary of Homeland Security

BENEFITS

• While in office, the president receives a salary of $400,000 each year. He or she lives in the White House and has 24-hour Secret Service protection.

• The president may travel on a Boeing 747 jet called Air Force One. The airplane can accommodate 70 passengers. It has kitchens, a dining room, sleeping areas, and a conference room. It also has fully equipped offices with the latest communications systems. Air Force One can fly halfway around the world before needing to refuel. It can even refuel in flight!

• If the president wishes to travel by car, he or she uses Cadillac One. Cadillac One is a Cadillac Deville. It has been modified with heavy armor and communications systems. The president takes Cadillac One along when visiting other countries if secure transportation will be needed.

• The president also travels on a helicopter called Marine One. Like the presidential car, Marine One accompanies the president when traveling abroad if necessary.

• Sometimes, the president needs to get away and relax with family and friends. Camp David is the official presidential retreat. It is located in the cool, wooded mountains in Maryland. The U.S. Navy maintains the retreat, and the U.S. Marine Corps keeps it secure. The camp offers swimming, tennis, golf, and hiking.

• When the president leaves office, he or she receives Secret Service protection for ten more years. He or she also receives a yearly pension of $191,300 and funding for office space, supplies, and staff.

PRESIDENTS AND THEIR TERMS

PRESIDENT	PARTY	TOOK OFFICE	LEFT OFFICE	TERMS SERVED	VICE PRESIDENT
George Washington	None	April 30, 1789	March 4, 1797	Two	John Adams
John Adams	Federalist	March 4, 1797	March 4, 1801	One	Thomas Jefferson
Thomas Jefferson	Democratic-Republican	March 4, 1801	March 4, 1809	Two	Aaron Burr, George Clinton
James Madison	Democratic-Republican	March 4, 1809	March 4, 1817	Two	George Clinton, Elbridge Gerry
James Monroe	Democratic-Republican	March 4, 1817	March 4, 1825	Two	Daniel D. Tompkins
John Quincy Adams	Democratic-Republican	March 4, 1825	March 4, 1829	One	John C. Calhoun
Andrew Jackson	Democrat	March 4, 1829	March 4, 1837	Two	John C. Calhoun, Martin Van Buren
Martin Van Buren	Democrat	March 4, 1837	March 4, 1841	One	Richard M. Johnson
William H. Harrison	Whig	March 4, 1841	April 4, 1841	Died During First Term	John Tyler
John Tyler	Whig	April 6, 1841	March 4, 1845	Completed Harrison's Term	Office Vacant
James K. Polk	Democrat	March 4, 1845	March 4, 1849	One	George M. Dallas
Zachary Taylor	Whig	March 5, 1849	July 9, 1850	Died During First Term	Millard Fillmore

PRESIDENT	PARTY	TOOK OFFICE	LEFT OFFICE	TERMS SERVED	VICE PRESIDENT
Millard Fillmore	Whig	July 10, 1850	March 4, 1853	Completed Taylor's Term	Office Vacant
Franklin Pierce	Democrat	March 4, 1853	March 4, 1857	One	William R.D. King
James Buchanan	Democrat	March 4, 1857	March 4, 1861	One	John C. Breckinridge
Abraham Lincoln	Republican	March 4, 1861	April 15, 1865	Served One Term, Died During Second Term	Hannibal Hamlin, Andrew Johnson
Andrew Johnson	Democrat	April 15, 1865	March 4, 1869	Completed Lincoln's Second Term	Office Vacant
Ulysses S. Grant	Republican	March 4, 1869	March 4, 1877	Two	Schuyler Colfax, Henry Wilson
Rutherford B. Hayes	Republican	March 3, 1877	March 4, 1881	One	William A. Wheeler
James A. Garfield	Republican	March 4, 1881	September 19, 1881	Died During First Term	Chester Arthur
Chester Arthur	Republican	September 20, 1881	March 4, 1885	Completed Garfield's Term	Office Vacant
Grover Cleveland	Democrat	March 4, 1885	March 4, 1889	One	Thomas A. Hendricks
Benjamin Harrison	Republican	March 4, 1889	March 4, 1893	One	Levi P. Morton
Grover Cleveland	Democrat	March 4, 1893	March 4, 1897	One	Adlai E. Stevenson
William McKinley	Republican	March 4, 1897	September 14, 1901	Served One Term, Died During Second Term	Garret A. Hobart, Theodore Roosevelt

PRESIDENT	PARTY	TOOK OFFICE	LEFT OFFICE	TERMS SERVED	VICE PRESIDENT
Theodore Roosevelt	Republican	September 14, 1901	March 4, 1909	Completed McKinley's Second Term, Served One Term	Office Vacant, Charles Fairbanks
William Taft	Republican	March 4, 1909	March 4, 1913	One	James S. Sherman
Woodrow Wilson	Democrat	March 4, 1913	March 4, 1921	Two	Thomas R. Marshall
Warren G. Harding	Republican	March 4, 1921	August 2, 1923	Died During First Term	Calvin Coolidge
Calvin Coolidge	Republican	August 3, 1923	March 4, 1929	Completed Harding's Term, Served One Term	Office Vacant, Charles Dawes
Herbert Hoover	Republican	March 4, 1929	March 4, 1933	One	Charles Curtis
Franklin D. Roosevelt	Democrat	March 4, 1933	April 12, 1945	Served Three Terms, Died During Fourth Term	John Nance Garner, Henry A. Wallace, Harry S. Truman
Harry S. Truman	Democrat	April 12, 1945	January 20, 1953	Completed Roosevelt's Fourth Term, Served One Term	Office Vacant, Alben Barkley
Dwight D. Eisenhower	Republican	January 20, 1953	January 20, 1961	Two	Richard Nixon
John F. Kennedy	Democrat	January 20, 1961	November 22, 1963	Died During First Term	Lyndon B. Johnson
Lyndon B. Johnson	Democrat	November 22, 1963	January 20, 1969	Completed Kennedy's Term, Served One Term	Office Vacant, Hubert H. Humphrey
Richard Nixon	Republican	January 20, 1969	August 9, 1974	Completed First Term, Resigned During Second Term	Spiro T. Agnew, Gerald Ford

PRESIDENT	PARTY	TOOK OFFICE	LEFT OFFICE	TERMS SERVED	VICE PRESIDENT
Gerald Ford	Republican	August 9, 1974	January 20, 1977	Completed Nixon's Second Term	Nelson A. Rockefeller
Jimmy Carter	Democrat	January 20, 1977	January 20, 1981	One	Walter Mondale
Ronald Reagan	Republican	January 20, 1981	January 20, 1989	Two	George H.W. Bush
George H.W. Bush	Republican	January 20, 1989	January 20, 1993	One	Dan Quayle
Bill Clinton	Democrat	January 20, 1993	January 20, 2001	Two	Al Gore
George W. Bush	Republican	January 20, 2001	January 20, 2009	Two	Dick Cheney
Barack Obama	Democrat	January 20, 2009			Joe Biden

"I leave you hoping that the lamp of liberty will burn in your bosoms until there shall no longer be a doubt that all men are created free and equal." Abraham Lincoln

WRITE TO THE PRESIDENT

You may write to the president at:

The White House
1600 Pennsylvania Avenue NW
Washington, DC 20500

You may e-mail the president at:

comments@whitehouse.gov

GLOSSARY

amendment - a change to a country's constitution.

assassinate - to murder a very important person, usually for political reasons.

Black Hawk War - in 1832, a conflict between Native Americans and the U.S. government over contested land in Illinois.

conscription - forced enrollment by law in a country's armed forces.

Constitution - the laws that govern the United States.

Constitutional Union Party - a short-lived political party formed in 1859. The party supported the Union, yet it ignored the slavery issue.

debate - a contest in which two sides argue for or against something.

Democrat - a member of the Democratic political party. When Abraham Lincoln was president, Democrats supported farmers and landowners.

deputy county surveyor - an official who works under a county surveyor. A surveyor is a person who measures a piece of land to determine its shape, area, and boundaries.

ferry - to carry across a body of water in a boat or other craft.

inaugurate (ih-NAW-gyuh-rayt) - to swear into a political office.

Mexican War - from 1846 to 1848. A war between the United States and Mexico.

militia (muh-LIH-shuh) - a group of citizens trained for war or emergencies.

postmaster - someone in charge of a post office.

precinct - a smaller part of a county or a town used in elections.

ratify - to officially approve.

Reconstruction - the period after the American Civil War when laws were passed to help the Southern states rebuild and return to the Union.

Republican - a member of the Republican political party. When Abraham Lincoln was president, Republicans supported business and strong government.

running mate - a candidate running for a lower-rank position on an election ticket, especially the candidate for vice president.

secede - to break away from a group.

Union - relating to the states that remained in the United States during the American Civil War.

Whig - a member of a political party that was very strong in the early 1800s but ended in the 1850s. Whigs supported laws that helped business.

WEB SITES

To learn more about Abraham Lincoln, visit ABDO Publishing Company on the World Wide Web at **www.abdopublishing.com**. Web sites about Abraham Lincoln are featured on our Book Links page. These links are routinely monitored and updated to provide the most current information available.

INDEX

A

American Civil War 4, 19, 20, 21, 22, 23, 24, 26, 27, 28, 29

assassination 4, 28, 29

B

Bell, John 17

Berry, William 11

birth 8

Black Hawk War 11

Booth, John Wilkes 28, 29

Breckinridge, John C. 17

C

childhood 4, 8, 9

Confederate States of America 19, 20, 21, 22, 24, 26, 27, 28

Confiscation Acts 20

Constitution, U.S. 22

Constitutional Union Party 17

Crittenden Compromise 19

D

death 28, 29

Democratic Party 16, 17, 26

deputy county surveyor 11

Douglas, Stephen A. 16, 17

E

education 4, 8, 9, 12

Emancipation Proclamation 22, 23

F

family 4, 8, 9, 10, 12, 13, 15, 19, 28

Ford's Theatre 28

Fort Sumter 19

G

Gettysburg, Battle of 24

Gettysburg Address 24

Grant, Ulysses S. 21, 26, 27

H

Hamlin, Hannibal 17

House of Representatives, U.S. 4, 14

I

Illinois legislator 4, 12

inauguration 19, 27

J

Johnson, Andrew 26

L

Lee, Robert E. 27

Lincoln-Douglas debates 17

M

McClellan, George B. 26

Mexican War 14

military service 11

N

Nevada 24

New Salem postmaster 11

P

Pendleton, George H. 26

Polk, James K. 14

R

Reconstruction 27

Republican Party 15, 16, 17, 18, 26

S

secession 18, 19, 22, 24

slavery 4, 14, 15, 16, 17, 18, 19, 20, 22, 23, 27, 29

T

Thirteenth Amendment 27

U

Union Party 26

W

West Virginia 24

Whig Party 12, 15

Wilmot Proviso 15